New Vanguard • 132

# Ancient Greek Warship

500–322 BC

Nic Fields • Illustrated by Peter Bull

First published in Great Britain in 2007 by Osprey Publishing,
Midland House, West Way, Botley, Oxford OX2 0PH, UK
443 Park Avenue South, New York, NY 10016, USA
E-mail: info@ospreypublishing.com



A CIP catalogue record for this book is available from the British Library

ISBN: 978 1 84603 074 1

Page layout by Melissa Orrom Swan, Oxford
Index by Margaret Vaudrey
Typeset in Helvetica Neue and ITC New Baskerville
Originated by PPS Grasmere Ltd, Leeds, UK
Printed in China through Worldprint Ltd.

07 08 09 10 11 10 9 8 7 6 5 4 3 2 1

For a catalogue of all books published by Osprey Military and Aviation please contact:

NORTH AMERICA
Osprey Direct, c/o Random House Distribution Center, 400 Hahn Road, Westminster, MD 21157
E-mail: info@ospreydirect.com

ALL OTHER REGIONS
Osprey Direct UK, P.O. Box 140 Wellingborough, Northants, NN8 2FA, UK
E-mail: info@ospreydirect.co.uk

**www.ospreypublishing.com**

## Artist's note

Readers may care to note that the original paintings from which the colour plates in this book were prepared are available for private sale. All reproduction copyright whatsoever is retained by the Publishers. All enquiries should be addressed to:

Peter Bull Art Studio, 8 Hurstwood Road, Bredhurst, Gillingham, Kent, ME7 3JZ

The Publishers regret that they can enter into no correspondence upon this matter.

## Abbreviations

A list of titles referred to in the text.

*FGrHist* – F. Jacoby, *Die Fragmente der griechischen Historiker*, Berlin & Leiden, (1923–)

Fornara – C. W. Fornara, *Translated Documents of Greece and Rome I: Archaic Times to the end of the Peloponnesian War*[2], Cambridge (1983)

Harding – P. Harding, *Translated Documents of Greece and Rome 2: From the end of the Peloponnesian War to the battle of Ipsus*, Cambridge (1985)

*IG* – *Inscriptiones Graecae*, Berlin (1923–)

## Glossary

| | |
|---|---|
| *Anakrousis* | Backing water – tactical manoeuvre |
| *Artemon* | 'Boat' sail |
| *Askōma/askōmata* | Leather sleeve for oar-port |
| *Aulētēs* | Double-pipe player |
| Cubit | Unit of length (Attic = 0.45m, Doric = 0.49m) |
| *Diekplous* | 'Through and out' – tactical manoeuvre |
| *Elatē* | Silver fir |
| *Embolos* | Ram |
| *Epibatēs/epibatai* | Marine |
| *Epiteichismoi* | Land bases near enemy territories |
| *Epōtis/epōtides* | Ear-timber |
| *Hoplitēs/hoplitai* | 'Fully-armed man' – hoplite |
| *Hypēresia* | 'Auxiliary group' – 14 armed men and 16 specialist seamen |
| *Hypersion* | Cushion |
| *Hypozōma/hypozōmata* | Rope under-belt |
| *Katastroma* | Deck |
| *Kedros* | Cedar |
| *Keleustēs* | Bo'sun |
| *Kōpai* | Oars |
| *Kubernētēs* | Helmsman |
| *Kuklos* | 'Circle' – defensive manoeuvre |
| *Kuparissos* | Cypress |
| Mortise | Recess cut to receive a tenon (q.v.) |
| *Naupēgos* | Shipwright |
| *Nautēs/nautai* | Oarsman |
| *Nautikon* | Navy; fleet |
| *Oiax/oiākos* | Tiller |
| *Parexeiresia* | 'Along-outside-rowing' – outrigger |
| *Perineō* | Spares (refers to oars and supernumerary personnel) |
| *Periplous* | 'Around' – tactical manoeuvre |
| *Peukē* | Mountain pine |
| *Pitys* | Coastal pine (larch) |
| *Platanos* | Plane |
| *Prōratēs* | Bow officer |
| *Skalmos/skalmoi* | Tholepin |
| Tenon | Hardwood rectangular block, each half-length fitting into a mortise (q.v.) |
| *Thalamia* | Oar ports |
| *Thalamioi* | Hold rowers |
| *Thalamos* | Ship's hold |
| *Thranitai* | Stool rowers |
| *Toxotēs/toxotai* | Archer |
| *Triērarchos/triērarchoi* | Sea-captain |
| *Triērēs/triērēis* | Trireme |
| *Zugioi* | Thwart rowers |

# ANCIENT GREEK WARSHIP 500–322 BC

## INTRODUCTION

During the classical period triremes (Greek *triērēs*, Latin *triremis*) were the most formidable and sophisticated warships in the Mediterranean. They were galleys designed to fight under oar power, although two square sails were provided for cruising – a main sail supplied the lift, while a 'boat' sail was used for steering. As no triremes survive, many aspects of their construction and operation are hotly disputed, especially the arrangement of the oars. However, they were long enough to allow files of about 30 rowers to row efficiently, which requires a length of about 35m (115ft), and this measurement corresponds well with the lengths of ancient ship sheds excavated at Peiraieus, the port of Athens. The ram is generally considered to have been their main armament, although boarding an enemy vessel with a view to deciding the issue by hand-to-hand combat was also an important tactic.

The Greek naval victory over the Persians at Salamis (480 BC) allowed the Athenians to develop a naval arm that would be used to 'liberate' the Greeks from Persian rule and create a maritime empire. While this maritime empire was based mainly around the Aegean and the Propontis (Sea of Marmara), an area Athens was to dominate for the greater part of the 5th century BC, its navy also enabled it to strike as far as Cyprus and Egypt, the last some 1,400km (756 nautical miles) away by sea. Triremes were to play an important role throughout the next great conflict in the

*Olympias* under oars off Porus in 1992. This full-scale reconstruction of an Athenian trireme follows the original sophisticated construction, with flushed planks attached to an internal framework and keel, stem- and stern-post. The main source of propulsion for this narrow, shallow and elegant vessel was oar power. (Author's collection)

Attic Late Geometric IIA (735–720 BC) spouted krater from Thebes depicting the abduction of Helen by Paris. Paris' vessel is a warship with oars apparently at two levels. The bireme was developed by the Phoenicians and later adopted by the Greeks. (London, British Museum, GR 1899.2-19.1, author's collection)

eastern Mediterranean, the Peloponnesian War (431–404 BC). This was the grand struggle between Athens and its allies on the one hand, and Sparta and its allies on the other. The trireme was the weapon by which Athens achieved and maintained power, but when the Athenians finally lost the contest in the Great Harbour at Syracuse, Sicily in 413 BC, it was partly because the trireme had lost the power to overawe its enemies.

# ORIGINS

Hipponax of Ephesos (*fl.* 550 BC) is the first Greek to mention the trireme. He urges the painter Mimnes 'not to go on painting a snake on the many-benched side of a *triērēs*, so that it seems to be running away from the ram towards the helmsman' (fr. 45 Diehl[3]). The Athenian historian Thucydides says (1.13.2) that the Corinthians were the first of the Greeks to build triremes, sometime around 700 BC.

Bas-relief from the palace of Sennacherib, Nineveh (c.701 BC) showing a Phoenician warship with a pointed forefoot sheathed in metal as a ram, and rowed at two levels. Yet the open topside could accommodate a third file of oarsmen and thus represents the earliest trireme. (Esther Carré)

A scaled wooden model of a Phoenician warship based on those depicted in the Nineveh bas-relief. Noted for their seafaring and shipbuilding skills, the Phoenicians are credited by ancient authors with the invention of the trireme. (Haifa, National Maritime Museum, Esther Carré)

According to Clement of Alexander (*Stromateis* 1.16.76), the invention of the trireme (or *trikrotos naus* in his Byzantine Greek), should be attributed to the seafaring Phoenicians, the foremost mariners of antiquity and recorded as such in the Bible (1 Kings 9: 27, Ezekiel 27: 4). A Nineveh bas-relief from the palace of Sennacherib reinforces this conclusion. The sculptor of this piece of Assyrian artwork, which illustrates the evacuations of Tyre and Sidon by King Lulī in 701 BC, credits the Phoenicians with a type of galley remarkably similar to a trireme.

The main piece of visual evidence for the Athenian trireme is the Lenormant relief from the Acropolis. Dating from the end of the 5th century BC, this fragmentary relief shows the mid-section of the starboard side of a trireme under oar, with the lowest oars emerging from oar-ports through leather sleeves (*askōmata*), the next level of oars emerging from under the outrigger, and the uppermost oars working through parallel timbers of the outrigger.

**Silver springs**

Xenophon believed that silver, along with Athens' natural produce and its central position by land and by sea, was 'the gift … of divine providence' (*Poroi* 1.5). In 483 BC, according to both Herodotos and Aristotle, Athens had the good fortune to find a new vein of silver, worth some 100 talents (approximately 26kg/57lb or 6,000 Attic *drachmae*), in the Laureion mines of south-east Attica. The mines were state-owned and, under normal conditions, the profits from them would have been shared out among the citizens. Yet on the proposal of Themistokles, the farsighted statesman and mainspring of Athens' naval ambitions, the Athenians voted to use this unexpected windfall to construct a navy. In its war with Aigina in 490 BC, for example, Athens could only summon 70 warships after 'they asked the Corinthians to lend them ships' (Herodotos 6.89). On the eve of Xerxes' invasion a decade later in 481 BC, however, Athens had at least 200 triremes ready for service (Herodotos 8.1.1, 14.1, 44.1).

It was these Athenian triremes that formed the bulk of the naval arm of the Hellenic League (the modern term for those Greek states who opposed Xerxes), and thus were to play a vital part in the victory at

Salamis. The Athenian tragedian Aischylos (born *c*.525 BC) uses the Persian chorus of his play, the *Persians* (*Persai*) to lament, with solemn emphasis, Athenian wealth and strength: 'silver springs run through their soil, a treasure from the earth for them' (238). Thucydides describes vividly the attitude of Athens' allies after Salamis. They feared 'the size of Athens' navy, which was not previously in existence, and the aggressive spirit it had shown in the face of the Persian attack' (1.90.1). Elsewhere, he remarks that immediately after the Persian wars the Athenians 'had begun to practise the art of seamanship' (1.142.7). There can be no doubt now that Athens was set to become the greatest sea power in the Greek world.

Washery #4 at Thorikos, looking west-south-west from Velatouri. The silver mines of Laureion, south-east Attica, had been exploited to a limited extent since the Bronze Age. In time, rich beds of ore were discovered lying deep below the surface, especially at Maroneia in 483 BC. (Author's collection)

# DESIGN

The Athenian trireme was a pre-industrial artefact pushed to the limit of what was technically possible at the time. It was a fragile warship, essentially designed to be highly manoeuvrable and capable of being driven by oars at high speed for short periods in battle.

### Oar system

The orthodox theory is that the trireme had six fore-and-aft files of oarsmen in a three-level arrangement (Morrison-Coates 133–137). Yet a radically different hypothesis promotes the idea that the trireme had only three files of oarsmen in all, rather than three either side, arranged at two, not three, levels (Tilley 2004).

Although controversy still surrounds the trireme, certain factors are clear. It was rowed at three levels with one man to each oar. The last fact is supported by a chance remark by Thucydides, who noted that each oarsman of a Corinthian trireme 'carried his oar, his cushion and his oar-loop' (2.93.2) across the isthmus between the Gulf of Corinth and the Saronic Gulf. Aischylos says the Greek triremes that fought at Salamis were *triskalmos*, 'with three tholepins' (*Persai* 679, 1074). A tholepin (*skalmos*) is the fulcrum for an oar, and took the form of a fixed vertical peg. In the Mediterranean the practice was, and still is, to use only one

The Lenormant relief, dated *circa* 410 BC, showing the mid-section of the starboard side of a trireme under oar. Delicately cut in local pink marble, the visible oarsmen are the *thranitai*, while two lower levels of oars emerge from the ship's side. (Athens, Acropolis Museum, 1339, author's collection)

tholepin for each oar, and to lash the oar to it with an oar-loop, in contrast to the practice of northern seamen, who prefer to use tholepins in pairs, with the oar working between them. The oar-loop, according to Homer (*Odyssey* 4.782), was made of leather, perhaps a strap sewn into a loop.

We learn from the Naval Inventories, a fragmentary series of 4th-century Athenian inscriptions (*IG* 2² 1604–1632) excavated in the ancient naval dockyard at Peiraieus, that these oars (*kōpai*) came in two slightly different lengths, 9 cubits (4.4m/14ft 5in.) and 9.5 cubits (4.6m/15ft) long (*IG* 2² 1606.43–44, 1607.14). Aristotle (*De natura animalium* 687b18) enlightens us here, explaining that those oars used towards the ends of the ship were shorter than those towards the middle.

The ancient Greek oarsmen rowed from a simple fixed seat, and to prevent blisters sat on a leather cushion (*hypersion*). In the *Frogs*, Aristophanes has a scene in which Charon forces the god Dionysos to row across the Styx, resulting in the god suffering from blisters on his backside, presumably because he did not have the luxury of a cushion.

*Thranitai* station on *Olympias*. In the hot and narrow space below the decks, the oarsmen probably wore little more than loincloths. As can be seen, the *thranitai* at least had a little fresh air, as well as the dubious luxury of a view through the open-sided outrigger. (Author's collection)

### Ship dimensions

Since triremes have positive buoyancy, no recognizable remains have been found on the seabed. The most important surviving relics, however, are the excavated ship sheds in Peiraieus, the port of Athens. These were buildings, built on the limestone bedrock and incorporating a slipway with a 1 in 10 gradient, up which triremes were normally hauled up when not at sea. Their remains provide evidence for the maximum dimensions for the Athenian ships: the overall length could not have been more than about 40m (131ft), and the beam at the widest point no more than about 6m (20ft).

It is also known that the horizontal distance between oarsmen was 'a space of two cubits' (Vitruvius 1.2.4). The number of oarsmen in the longest fore-and-aft file of a trireme is known from the Naval Inventories to be 31. With a Doric cubit equivalent to 49cm (19in.), the length of the rowing area of the ship was about 30m (98ft) and hence the length of the whole ship some 37m (120ft), a perfect fit for the ship sheds in Peiraieus.

Remains of two ship sheds at Sounion. This rock-cut chamber within the fortifications contains two short narrow slips to house scout ships. The slips are just over 21m (68ft) long, 2.6m (8ft 6in.) wide, narrowing to 1.15m (3ft 8in.), cut deep into the rock and very steep, with a 1 in 3.5 slope. (Author's collection)

## CONSTRUCTION

Triremes were light enough to be manhandled. There is a 5th-century inscription (*IG* 1³ 153) to the effect that 140 men were used to carry a trireme up a ship shed's slipway and 120 to get her down. Aristophanes, in his comedy *Knights* acted in Athens in 424 BC, has a trireme speak to her comrades-in-arms, saying, 'I, like you, am built of pine and joinery' (1310). Such lightweight carpentry required skilled shipwrights.

### Hull

In northern Europe most wooden hulls have been made by a method called 'clinker'. The keel was first laid down, with a heavy, shaped beam

The keel of *Olympias*. At night, whenever possible, triremes would be dragged up the beach stern first. Hence the keel, which was made of oak, was a substantial girder on the middle line of the vessel. (Author's collection)

('keelson') on top of it, and the stem- and stern-post joined to it. Then vertical frames were attached at intervals, which determined the eventual shape of the hull. The outside shell of planks was then put on, starting with one either side of the keelson ('garboards') each overlapping the one below by a small amount.

The eastern Mediterranean tradition of shipbuilding was known as 'carvel' construction. The hull itself was made up of keel, stem- and stern-post, frames, planks, gunwales and beams. The longitudinal members were put together by use of mortise-and-tenon joints fixed by dowel-pins – brilliantly described by Homer in his quintessential sailor's story, the *Odyssey* (5.248, 361) – and covered by a stressed carvel-built shell of planks, which were fixed edge-to-edge rather than overlapping, to give a smoother, faster hull. The usual practice was to shape and fit the ribs inside the hull after it was completed – the reverse order of construction from that of a clinker-built boat.

To strengthen and protect a hull made in this way from rough seas, the Greeks used devices called 'under-belts' (*hypozōmata*). These were probably heavy ropes fitted low down in the ship and stretched by means of windlasses from stem to stern. In the Naval Inventories four are the norm for each ship, while six are taken on distant missions (*IG* $2^2$ 1629.11). Indeed when a trireme was in commission she was often described as 'girded', that is, with the *hypozōmata* fitted (*IG* $2^2$ 1627.29). An earlier Athenian inscription (*IG* $1^3$ 153), dating to around 440 BC, gives a decree prescribing the minimum number of men (probably 50) allowed to rig a *hypozōma*. It is clear that considerable tension was required. Apollonios of Rhodes, describing the building of the *Argo*, says that the Argonauts 'first girded the ship mightily with a well twisted rope from within, putting a tension on each end so that the planks should fit well with the tenons and should withstand the opposing forces of the sea surge' (*Voyage of Argo* 1.367–369).

## Materials

The trireme was not a 'heart of oak'. For lightness combined with strength, ship-timber was mostly of softwoods such as pine and fir. Plato, who deplored the effects of a maritime economy on a city's life, makes the Athenian stranger ask a question natural to an Athenian: 'How is the environment of our colonial city off for ship-timber?' He gets the answer: 'There is no fir (*elatē*) to speak of, nor pine (*peukē*), and not much cypress (*kuparissos*); nor is much larch (*pitys*) or plane (*platanos*) to be found, which shipwrights normally have to use for the inner parts of ships.' (*Laws* 705C)

Theophrastos, a younger contemporary of Plato and a pupil of Aristotle, lists the three principal ship timbers as fir, pine and cedar (*kedros*), the last having become more readily available from Syria as a result of Alexander's conquests. Beforehand he had compared the fir and the pine: 'The latter is fleshier and has few fibres, while the former has many fibres and is not fleshy. That is why the pine is heavy and the fir light. Triremes … are made of fir for the sake of lightness.' (*Enquiry* 5.1.5)

Elsewhere (*Enquiry* 5.4.4), Theophrastes says pine is second-best timber for triremes because it is heavier. Earlier, regarding wood for the internal structure, he says: 'Sometimes the internal parts of triremes are made of larch as well, because of its light weight. But the stem-posts, which adjoin the breastwork, and the bow timbers, are made of ash and mulberry and elm, since these parts have to be tough.' (*Enquiry* 4.2.8) The emphasis on lightness for the timber for the hull and for the rest of a trireme is obviously a prime consideration in its overall design. One 4th century BC trireme is called by the name *Kouphotatē* – Lightness (*IG* 2² 1629.1).

The woods were not plentiful at all times in Greece, and the Athenians imported large quantities mainly from Macedonia and Thrace. A string of treaties with Macedonian kings guaranteed Athens' right to import high-quality timber from Macedon or to send its shipwrights there to build ships on the spot, thus saving the costly transport of timber by sea (*IG* 1³ 89, 117, 182). Speaking of a Syracusan shipbuilding programme of 399 BC, Diodoros (14.42.4) mentions the procurement of good quality pine and fir from Italy.

One result of using softwoods was that the hull of a trireme tended to soak up water. Consequently, all triremes were beached and carried out of the water as often as possible to dry and clean the hulls. One of the most serious problems for the Athenians besieging Syracuse in 414 BC was that the enemy was able to launch its ships at any time it chose, whereas the Athenians, having no reserve of vessels, had to keep all theirs constantly in the water in case of a sudden attack. As a result, their hulls became waterlogged, and they could not make anything like their maximum speed (Thucydides 7.12–13).

The top deck and gangway on *Olympias*. On an Athenian trireme the top deck was a flimsy affair, a narrow wooden canopy open in the centre for a gangway that ran from the quarterdeck to bow. There was no deck rail. (Author's collection)

The fixed seats on *Olympias.* Every oarsman had a cushion – perhaps a seat pad made of sheepskin – and was doubtless assigned a regular seat on board. This would allow him to get used to the timing of the men around him and to adjust his stroke accordingly. (Author's collection)

The hulls would not only become waterlogged and leaky, but they would also suffer from that scourge of wooden ships, the naval borer (Greek *terēdōn*, Latin *teredo navalis*), the maritime equivalent of woodworm or deathwatch beetle. Ancient shipwrights avoided using certain woods for the hull because they were thought to be susceptible to it, larch particularly so according to the elder Pliny (*Naturalis historia* 16.79).

Oars were a vital part of a trireme's gear. In Homer 'shaved fir' (*Iliad* 7.5, *Odyssey* 12.172) is a synonym for oars, and each oar-shaft was made from a rough, young fir-tree, very carefully prepared (Theophrastos *Enquiry* 5.1.6–7). Stripping coaxial layers from saplings ensured that the grain of the wood was aligned along the shaft, making the oars strong for their weight. The Naval Inventories show how carefully the oars were inspected for faults, and those that were sub-standard were rejected. The procurement of suitable oar-timber was important to Athens. Thrace, in which Athens had a continuing interest throughout the period of its naval ascendancy, is noted by Herodotos as 'having much ship-timber and many oar-shafts and silver mines' (5.23.2). Perdikkas, the king of Macedon (d. 413 BC), signed a treaty with Athens, probably during the Peloponnesian War, engaging himself to export Macedonian oar timber, at the discount price of 5 *drachmae* apiece, to Athens alone (*IG* 1³ 89.31, 117, 182).

Once at Peiraieus, naval supplies were protected by an export ban. We know, from a casual remark in Aristophanes' the *Frogs* (364), of a prohibition on the shipment overseas of the sailcloth, pitch, and of *askōmata* that kept water out of the lowest oar-ports, but restrictions of this sort would have applied to all other items.

### Decoration

After 'swift', the most common epithet Homer uses for ships is 'black', the blackness being the result of applications of pine pitch on ships' hulls to make them watertight. The same is true of Athenian triremes. In his play the *Acharnians*, Aristophanes has an envoy return from Sparta

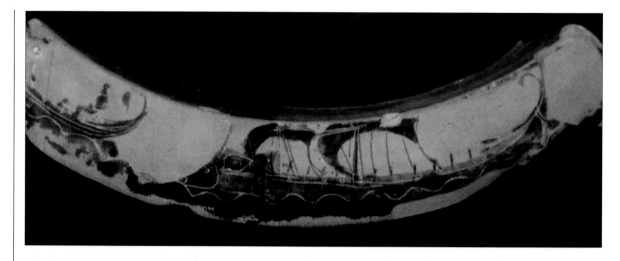

Fragment of a Corinthian black-figure krater, dated to the second-half of the 6th century BC. The Corinthians are credited with being the first Greeks to build triremes. This trireme has a ram in the shape of a goat's head with an apotropaic eye. (Corinth, Archaeological Museum, C 72-38, Esther Carré)

armed with a five-year truce, but the hero Dikaiopolis, who is keen to end the war, does not like it because 'it smells of pitch and naval preparations' (190). Ships were given a coat of pitch in preparation for an expedition. The substance is mentioned in one of the Naval Inventories (*IG* 2² 1622.740), where it is listed as part of the gear for a trireme, the *Amphitrite*.

Every Athenian trireme had a name. Warships were considered feminine (*IG* 2² 1609 = Harding 47). They were named for goddesses, like Artemis and Aphrodite; for sea-nymphs like Thetis and Amphitrite; for ideals, like Democracy, Freedom and Equality; for animals, like Lioness, Gazelle and Sea Horse; the quixotic, like Blameless, Fair Weather and Good Repute; and even for piratical notions like Rapine and Pillage. Of special note were the sacred (or state) triremes *Salaminia* and *Paralos*, two fast ships always fully manned and used for special missions such as carrying envoys (Thucydides 3.33.1). Every ship had an image depicting its name on a painted plaque attached to the prow. The name was possibly written out as well, but the painted image served several important purposes. It was relatively easy to identify in battle, it provided a symbol around which the crew could rally and, not least, it was comprehensible.

The prow of a trireme was often decorated to look like the head of an animal with the ram as its snout. Aischylos calls triremes 'the dark-eyed ships' (*Persai* 559, *Suppliants* 773). The eye – which is a regular decoration on prows of earlier oared ships – in the trireme was a piece of polished marble, shaped and painted to resemble an eye. Some have been discovered in Zea and provide an explanation of the enigmatic entries in one of the Naval Inventories that the eyes of a ship are 'broken' (*IG* 2² 1604.68), and in another that in a certain ship 'there is no gear and even the eyes are missing' (*IG* 2² 1607.24).

# CREW

'Why is a trireme, fully manned, such a terror to the enemy and a joy to her friends', asks Xenophon, 'except by reason of her speed through the water?' (*Oikonomikos* 8.8). In Xenophon's eyes the Athenian trireme's chief virtue was speed.

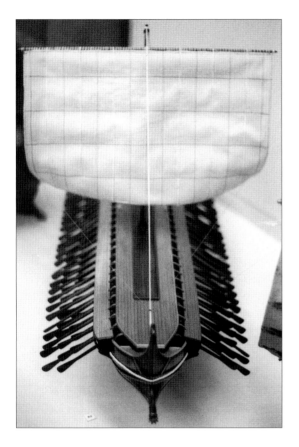

**Model of a trireme under sail. The main mast, seen here, is stepped about amidships. Although not shown, a second 'boat' mast was raked and stepped forward. Sails were either of papyrus ('light') or of flax ('heavy'), as were ropes. (Edinburgh, Royal Museum, T 1980.31, author's collection)**

## Oarsmen

In Athens the oarsmen were not slaves but highly trained professionals drawn from the fourth property class, the thetes, as defined by the constitution of the lawgiver Solon (*fl.* 595 BC). These men, the poorest Athenian citizens, nicknamed the 'naval mob' by Aristotle (*Politics* 1291b24, 1304a22), were renowned for their skills as seamen (Thucydides 1.80.4). According to the right-wing pamphleteer the 'Old Oligarch', 'the majority [of the thetes], can row as soon as they get aboard since they have practised throughout their lives' (Pseudo-Xenophon *Athenaion politeia* 1.20). Though written by an opponent of Athens' radical democracy, this is a view that accords well with the words Thucydides puts into the mouth of the Athenian statesman Perikles (d. 429 BC), namely 'sea power is a matter of skill … and it is not possible to get practise in the odd moment when the chance occurs, but is a full-time occupation, leaving no moment for other things' (1.142.9).

According to the Naval Inventories there were 27 oarsmen each side at the lowest level of the trireme, the *thalamioi*, or hold-rowers. These men worked their oars through oar-ports (*thalamia*). In the middle level there were 27 oarsmen each side, the *zugioi*, or thwart-rowers. At the top level there were 31 on each side, known as *thranitai*, or stool-rowers, who rowed through an outrigger (*parexeiresia*). This was an extension beyond the side of the trireme, which gave greater leverage to the oars. The other advantage in this arrangement was that the *thranitai* were to one side ('outboard') of those below them, which meant they did not have to be so far above them vertically. This lowered the centre of gravity, making the trireme more stable without increasing its beam. It also enabled them to use oars of the same length as those of the other two levels, without having to hold them at a very steep angle to the water. Even so, their task was considered the hardest.

These top level oarsmen, who as leaders of a 'triad' had a greater responsibility for synchronized rowing, were provided with bonuses on top of their daily wage. According to Thucydides 'the crews of the ships were all paid at the same rate' (3.17.4); before 413 BC this rate was paid at a *drachma* a day (6.31.3), but halved to 3 obols in the austere days in the aftermath of the Sicilian expedition (8.45.2). Only half the rate of a *drachma* a day was actually payable to Athenian crews while on active service; the rest became due when the ship was paid off in Peiraieus (Thucydides 8.45.2).

Although the oarsmen were protected to a certain degree from weather and in battle from enemy missiles by a light deck (*katastroma*), the trireme was open at the sides above the topwale. The Syracusans exploited this weakness in the early sea battles in the Great Harbour in 413 BC, when they employed skiffs to get close in among the Athenian ships from which missiles were thrown in among the oarsmen (Thucydides 7.40.5). There were side-screens (*pararrymata*) of canvas and hide among the gear

of triremes in the Naval Inventories (*IG* 2² 1605.40–43, 1609.85–87, 113, 1611.244–249, 1612.73–79, 1627.348). The hides were presumably for protection against such attacks, while the canvas provided protection against the elements. In Xenophon (*Hellenika* 2.1.22) vertical side-screens are hung over the outriggers before battle.

It must be said that the *thalamioi* had the most unpleasant and dangerous position. If the ship got badly holed, they were most likely to be drowned or captured by an enemy boarding party. Oarsmen were unarmed. Also, as Aristophanes (*Frogs* 1074) points out with rather plain vulgarity, they sat with their faces rather close to the backsides of the *zugioi* above and in front of them. They would have suffered also from the sweat of those above dripping down on them. Similarly, their oar-ports were only about 45cm (19in.) above the waterline, and even with efficient *askōmata*, they must have got quite wet.

To sum up, the three categories of oarsmen were as follows: 62 *thranitai*, or upper oarsmen; 54 *zugioi* or middle oarsmen; and 54 *thalamioi* or lower oarsmen, giving a total of 170 oarsmen. This is exactly the number of oars, not counting the 30 spares (*kōpai perineō*), supplied to an Athenian trireme (*IG* 2² 1607.9.19). The spares were carried on board in case of breakages among the 170 working oars.

## Deck crew

The full complement of a trireme was 200 (Herodotos 3.13.1–2, 7.184.1, 8.17, Thucydides 6.8, 8.29.2, Xenophon *Hellenika* 1.5.3–7), of whom 170 were the oarsmen. According to the Decree of Themistokles (Fornara 55), which apparently records the measures taken by the Athenian assembly in 481 BC to meet the threatened Persian invasion, the fighting men of an Athenian trireme included ten hoplites (*hoplitai*), enlisted as deck soldiers (*epibatai*) from men between the ages of 20 and 30, and four archers (*toxotai*) (lines 23–26). This practice appears to have continued throughout the 5th century BC (Thucydides 2.23.2, 3.94.1, 95.2), although 4th-century crew lists often give only two or three archers. One trireme, for example, had 11 *epibatai* and three *toxotai* (*IG* 2² 1951.82–84).

This left ten deckhands plus the sea captain (*triērarchos*), the helmsman (*kubernētēs*), the bow officer (*prōratēs*), the shipwright (*naupēgos*), the bo'sun (*keleustēs*, 'exhorter'), who controlled the oarsmen,

**Decree of Themistokles, 481 BC**
Known from the name of the politician who moved its passage in the Assembly of the People (*ekklesia*), the decree was the official state record of the provisions for meeting the expected Persian invasion. In 1959 M. H. Jameson re-discovered the decree at the back of a café in Troezen, north-eastern Peloponnese, and he published it the following year. Inscribed upon a marble stele with 3rd century BC lettering, the text is cut in the classical manner, *stoichēdon*, each letter below a letter of the preceding line, with 42 letters to a line. Obviously scholars fiercely contest the authenticity of this decree, although some, such as Lazenby (1993: 102–104) believe it to be a patriotic fabrication of the 4th century BC, put in its final form in the 3rd century, rather than a true copy of an official Athenian decree of 481 BC.

In short, Themistokles proposed that the Athenians and all foreigners (*metikoi*) who resided in Athens should send their women and children to Troezen, reputedly the birthplace of the Athenian hero-king Theseus. All able-bodied men of fighting age should then embark on the 200 triremes that had been prepared to fight the trousered 'long-haired Medes'. The Athenians committed themselves to resisting the Persians, and Themistokles' political acumen turned Xerxes' invasion into a people's war.

and a double-pipe player (*aulētēs*), who piped time for them (Pseudo-Xenophon *Athenaion politeia* 1.2, *IG* 2z 1951.94–105). Sometimes the oarsmen would join in a rhythmic cry, repeating it over and over to mark time. The cries '*O opop, O opop*' and '*ryppapai*', each one mimicking the rhythm of the oar stroke, are both attested for Athenian crews (Aristophanes, *Frogs* 208, 1073).

The *kubernētēs* was the highest-ranking professional seaman on a trireme, given that he was in complete charge of navigation under oar and sail. He made decisions, sometimes split-second decisions, which might provide the margin of victory in battle. He was assisted by the *keleustēs*, whose business was to manage the oarsmen and get the best out of them (Plato *Alkibiades* 1.125C, Xenophon *Oikonomikos* 21.3). The 14 armed men and the 16 officers and ratings were known collectively as the *hypēresia*, or auxiliary group. They are best seen as assistants to the *triērarchos*.

### Marines

According to Herodotos (6.15.2), the 100 Chiot triremes at Lade in 494 BC each carried 40 picked hoplites serving as *epibatai*. Herodotos (7.184.2) mentions that Persian triremes carried, in addition to native marines, 30 additional fighting men who were Persians, Medes or Sakai, the last of whom were a nomadic people of central Asia, highly valued for their archery skills. Every Persian ship was supplied by Persian subjects, including Phoenicians, Egyptians, Carians, Cypriots and Greeks, among others. The non-seafaring Persians supplied only admirals and marines.

The last were probably on board to ensure the loyalty of the ship's company and for that reason they were undoubtedly carried in battle.

The ten *epibatai* on an Athenian trireme had the highest status in the ship after the *triērarchos*. They are mentioned second in the Decree of Themistokles, and this is the position they occupy in the 4th-century crew lists (*IG* 2² 1951.79–82). Thucydides notes that they joined the *triērarchos* in pouring libations at the ceremonial departure of the Sicilian expedition (6.32.1).

One reason for the Athenian practice of taking only a few hoplites on deck to serve as marines was that the crew's pulling efficiency was seriously jeopardized if there were too many people moving about topside. Such movement inevitably caused the ship to roll. Under oar, therefore, the *epibatai* had to be seated (Thucydides 7.67.2), and the procedure appears to have been to keep them centred on the middle line of the ship. Once the vessel had stopped to board an enemy vessel, the *epibatai* would leap up to fight once the ships grappled. In his speech before the final sea battle in the Great Harbour at Syracuse, the Athenian commander Nikias revealed another reason: 'Many archers and javelineers will be on deck and a mass of hoplites, which we would not employ if

Attic red-figure krater from Nola (c.480 BC). A hoplite pours a libation to the gods before battle. He wears a linen corselet, and his Corinthian helmet is tilted back, as was customary when the hoplite was off the field. (London, British Museum, E 269, author's collection)

Attic black-figure platter fragment from the Acropolis of Athens (*c.*530 BC). The scene shows an oared warship carrying hoplites serving as *epibatai*. Though at the ready, these heavily armed men have to be careful not to shift position and unbalance the ship. (Athens, National Archaeological Museum 2414, author's collection)

we were fighting a battle in the open sea, because they would hinder us through the weight of the ships in exercising our skill.' (Thucydides 7.62.2) Weight, particularly on deck, prevented the triremes doing what they did best, namely, conducting the tactical manoeuvres in which speed and agility were essential.

### Archers

The four *toxotai* were distinct from the ten *epibatai*, namely they were not carried on deck. An inscription (*IG* $1^2$ 950.137), dated to 412/411 BC, gives them a descriptive adjective, *paredroi*, meaning 'sitting beside'. It

Proto-Corinthian olpe, the so-called Chigi Vase from Veii (*c.*650 BC). The scene depicts the collision of two hoplite phalanxes; the left-hand one includes a piper blowing a double pipe. Each pipe (*aulos*) was a cylinder with finger holes, sounded with a reed. (Rome, Villa Giulia 22679, author's collection)

seems that they were posted in the stern beside the *triērarchos* and *kubernētēs* and acted as their bodyguard in action. The helmsman would certainly have been vulnerable and would have needed protection, being too busy to defend himself. The Athenian playwright Euripides (*Iphigenia among the Taurians* 1377) talks of archers stationed in the stern, giving covering fire during an embarkation.

# IN ACTION

Lack of space in the hull for food and water, low freeboard, low cruising speed under oars and limited sailing qualities reduced the trireme's range of operations. Hence, naval engagements customarily took place near the coast, where ships could be handled in relatively calm water and there was some hope for the shipwrecked. Sails were used for fleets in transit, but when the ships approached the battle area, the masts would be lowered and the ships rowed. The opposing fleets normally deployed in line abreast two deep.

### Armament
The main weapon of a trireme was the bronze-plated ram (*embolos*) situated at the prow. In the *Persians* Aischylos speaks of the use of 'brazen rams' at Salamis (*Persai* 408, 415), and they appear in the Naval Inventories as returnable items when a ship is broken up (*IG* 2² 1623.113–123, 1628.498). The ram was formed by the forward tip of the keel, heavily armoured and built up to a point with three chisel-like blades just above water level. The join between the ram and the stern-post, which curved upwards and forwards, was shaped to reduce water resistance so that the whole structure acted both as an armament and as a cutwater.

Scythian archers appear on a number of Athenian vases, always clothed in patterned sleeved tunics and trousers, and soft leather caps, and often associated with horses. Here, on the interior of an Attic red-figure kylix, a *toxotēs* inspects one of his arrows. (Berlin, Staatiche Museen, F 2296, author's collection)

Before the invention of gunpowder (and long after) the offensive capabilities of warships were limited to setting an enemy vessel on fire, piercing the hull at the waterline or boarding. Advances in Greek warship design were aimed at achieving the speed necessary for successful ramming without loss of stability. Impact theory indicates that unless the attacker reached the critical speed of about 10 knots at the moment of impact, the attacking vessel would crumple, while the target vessel escaped almost unscathed. The oarsmen obviously needed to deliver a high strike rate, perhaps approaching 50 strokes per minute. Ominously the Greek word for stroke, *embolē*, is the same word used for 'charge' or 'ramming'.

The ram could smash a hole in an enemy vessel and so cripple her, but could not literally sink her. Ancient sources use terms meaning 'sink', but it is evident that ships so 'sunk' could still be towed away. The Greek word *kataduein*, which is almost invariably translated as 'sink', in fact means no more than 'dip' or 'lower'. So, when triremes were holed in a sea battle, although they had become absolutely useless as fighting vessels, the combatants went to great lengths and some risk to recover the wrecks. After the naval engagement off Sybota in 433 BC, the Corinthians did not take into tow the triremes they had put out of action, something Thucydides (1.50.1) implies that they could have done. Such vessels could be towed home as prizes and, after being repaired, equipped and re-named, they became part of the navy (*IG 2² 1606*).

## Naval tactics

There were two main methods of fighting, which placed contradictory demands on trireme design. The first was ramming, which called for the smallest possible ship built around the largest number of oarsmen. Using a minimum number of marines, the Athenian navy followed this philosophy. The second method was boarding, which required

larger, heavier ships capable of carrying the maximum number of boarders. The men of Chios, for example, with their 40 marines per trireme, opted for the second tactic. This is the style of attack which eventually prevailed, simply because a vessel had to make contact with its opponent when ramming, which was just what the boarders wanted. The later development of large ships with complete decks, specifically the warships of the Hellenistic period, which were primarily designed as heavily armoured floating platforms to carry either catapults or marines, was a logical progression.

The arguments of Herodotos (8.60) regarding why the Greeks fought in the narrow Salamis channel are worth examining in some detail. First, he noted that if Eurybiades, the Spartan admiral-in-chief, chose to give battle at the Isthmus of Corinth, this would mean fighting 'on the wide open sea'. Second, fighting in the open sea was 'least advantageous' to the Greeks with their 'heavier' (*barutéras*) and less numerous ships.

It is not at all clear what he meant by 'heavier' ships. It has been suggested (Morrison-Coates 2000: 153–154) that while Herodotos reports that the Persian triremes had been hauled ashore and dried out at Doriskos, those of the Greeks had become waterlogged through being continuously in the water for perhaps as long as a year. Nevertheless, there is no reason why the Greeks should not have dried their ships out, either before Artemision or in the interlude before Salamis, apart from the fact that Herodotos does not mention any attempt to do so.

Another possibility is that the Greek triremes were heavier in the sense that they were more heavily constructed. Thucydides (1.14.3) implies that although the Athenian triremes at Salamis were the most recently built in Greece, they were nevertheless old-fashioned in not having complete decks – there was a gap running down the centre of the top-deck. After Salamis, according to Plutarch, Kimon 'made them broader and put a bridge between their decks so that they might be able to attack the enemy in a more formidable fashion with many hoplites' (*Kimon* 12.2). It appears, on Plutarch's evidence at least, that post-Salamis Athenian triremes were completely decked.

It may well be that Greek triremes were, in other respects, not built as well as the best ships in the Persian navy, namely the Phoenician and Egyptian triremes. Ships built for speed and manoeuvrability were actually at a disadvantage in confined waters, and it is possible that Themistokles had realized this after Athenian experiences off Artemision. Indeed, at that engagement Herodotos implicitly says that the Persian vessels were 'better sailing' (8.10.1). What is more, he says (8.9) that the Persians were capable of carrying out the *diekplous*, a manoeuvre designed to row between the opposing ships and to turn hard about so as to ram an enemy vessel in the stern quarter. This suggests that the Persian crews were better trained than were those of Greek triremes.

The shape of the ram was designed to cause maximum waterline damage without penetrating the hull too far and making it difficult for the attacking vessel to back off. In *Olympias* the bronze sheath weighs some 200kg (440lb). (Author's collection)

**19**

Unfortunately Herodotos is very vague on the naval tactics employed by either side at Salamis (or Artemision). He does claim (8.11.1) that the Hellenic League fleet formed a defensive circle (*kuklos*) at the first engagement off Artemision, and this would indicate a defensive measure to counter the *diekplous*. However, with 271 triremes this circle would have been rather large to say the least, and one wonders if ships were capable of remaining in station in such a formation. Again, our knowledge of Salamis is limited with respect to battle tactics. The only real impression of the engagement from Herodotos is that it was a 'slogging match', and there are no indications of brilliant tactical moves being made by either navy.

To carry out the *diekplous* successfully required the open sea. The straits of Salamis are only about a mile wide and thus unsuitable for this tactic. Besides, if the heavier triremes of the Greeks meant they were more strongly built, then they could have better stood up to ramming. As we know, the Chiot triremes at Lade in 494 BC were packed with 40 hoplites acting as *epibatai* (Herodotos 6.15.2), which does suggest that the Greeks relied on boarding more than ramming. Likewise, in his scornful description of the sea battle of Sybota in 433 BC, Thucydides says the style of fighting had been 'of the old clumsy sort' (1.49.1). Here the triremes were carrying many hoplites and archers and the engagement 'had almost the appearance of a battle by land' (1.49.2) with both sides (apart from the small Athenian contingent) fighting 'with fury and brute strength rather than with skill' (1.49.3).

Whether boarding or ramming, ships had to collide, and this also limited their tactical capabilities. The trireme itself could be used as a weapon when ramming, but the problem was to avoid damaging one's own ship or becoming so entangled with the enemy vessel that boarding became inevitable. Yet speed and manoeuvrability could make it possible to attack vulnerable sides and sterns. For the Athenians, ramming head-on had come to be considered a sign of lack of skill in a helmsman (Thucydides 7.36.5), and the manoeuvre-and-ram school, in which the Athenian navy reigned supreme, relied on two tactical options, the *diekplous* and the *periplous*.

**Marble grave stele probably from Athens (c.380 BC) of Demokleides, who died at sea serving as an *epibatēs*. The pensive young man sits on the foredeck of the trireme in which he served, with his shield and helmet behind him. (Athens, National Archaeological Museum 752, author's collection)**

The *periplous* manoeuvre was either a variation involving outflanking the enemy line when there was plenty of sea room, or the final stage of the *diekplous*, when the manoeuvring vessel, having cut through the line, swung round to attack from the stern. Once the enemy formation had broken up, the *periplous* would have become the most important tactical option available to the helmsman (Thucydides 7.36.3, 4, Xenophon *Hellenika* 1.6.31).

It was a tactical manoeuvre that a single, skilfully handled vessel performed to make a ramming attack that did not involve prow-to-prow contact. Even so, it required room for its execution, and timing was of the essence. With a modest speed of 9 knots, each trireme, assailant and victim, would travel its own length in about 6.5 seconds. If the attacker arrived too soon, he could himself be struck and holed by the target vessel; too late and the speed of impact fell off rapidly and he could deliver no more than a mild bump.

**Ancient Salamis town (Kamateró), as seen from the Paloúkia–Pérama ferry. It was from the bay below that the bulk of the Greek fleet, the Athenians and the Corinthians, came out in columns of line-ahead. On reaching their appointed station, the triremes turned to port into lines abeam. (Author's collection)**

There were two counter-moves to the *diekplous* and *periplous*. The first, according to Thucydides, was to occupy a position that was crowded (7.36) or, if in open water, form the *kuklos*, a defensive circle with rams pointing outward (Thucydides 2.83.5, 3.78.1). The alternative, especially for a large fleet, was to form up in double line abeam (Xenophon *Hellenika* 1.6.28). The ships in the second line would try to pick off any enemy vessel that broke through before it could turn and ram a friendly vessel in the first line.

# RULING THE WAVES

Even if it is true, and we have no reason to doubt the facts given by Diodoros (14.41.3, 42.2, 44.7), that Dionysios I of Syracuse was responsible for the introduction of larger ships, such as the quadrireme (Greek *tetrērēs*, Latin *quadriremis*) and the quinquereme (Greek *pentērēs*, Latin *quinqueremis*), the principal warship of the period remained the trireme. Similarly, by the end of the 4th century BC more exotic weapons, such as catapults and fire-pots, came into use, yet the main armament of the trireme remained the bronze-sheathed ram. Ram-and-board, therefore, continued as the universal tactic of naval warfare.

### Limitations of sea power

The ability to ram made the trireme very effective in battle, but it was not very seaworthy. It was clearly designed to pack as many rowers as possible into a given length of hull, the aim being to drive the ship as fast as possible.

The trireme was accordingly light and comparatively frail, and was not equipped to endure rough weather for long, thus restricting its ability to remain at sea for any period of time. The Athenian trireme that sailed day and night from Peiraieus to Mytilene in the summer of 427 BC, a distance of 355km (192 nautical miles), was an exception rather than the norm (Thucydides 3.49). Normally a trireme would put into shore at the first sign of a storm, for the crew's midday meal and then again for the night. It was not necessary to find an anchorage; a beach was

good enough, for the same light construction that endangered the vessel in storms permitted it easily to be drawn up on shore. Xenophon's account (*Hellenika* 6.2.27–39) of Iphikrates' voyage around a hostile Peloponnese in the summer of 372 BC illustrates this point well.

Obviously, if a trireme had to put to shore twice a day, no navy was capable of blockading a single coastal state, let alone an island. The only effective naval strategy was to station fleets in close proximity and receive advance warning of any enemy shipping either approaching or leaving the objective, and then, with luck, intercept the target. Our primary sources provide examples of this *modus operandi* failing. Although the Athenians were masters of naval warfare, during the Sicilian expedition they failed to prevent seaborne reinforcements reaching Syracuse or to intercept a squadron of 12 Peloponnesian triremes despatched to reinforce the Syracusan navy (Thucydides 7.1–2, 7.1). Again, the Peloponnesian fleet blockading the Athenian fleet in the harbour of Mytilene failed to prevent Konon launching two fast triremes, which subsequently escaped the blockaders, 'who had been having their meal ashore' (Xenophon *Hellenika* 1.6.21), and reached the open sea.

Control of the seas in the modern sense was impossible for a trireme navy, and sea power, therefore, had distinct limitations. Nevertheless, it did allow a maritime state to strike at very great distances; Athens could reach as far as southern Italy, Cyprus or Egypt, the last location being some 1,400km (870 miles) from Peiraieus. Much closer to home, Athens could raid up and down the Peloponnesian coast. Tolmides did so during the summer of 456 BC, burning the Spartan dockyards at Gytheion, capturing Corinthian Chalkis and, 'after making a landing at Sikyon, defeated the Sikyonians in battle' (Thucydides 1.108.5).

Still, unless admirals were prepared to risk their hoplites ashore, as Tolmides evidently was, they were limited as to what they could achieve. As far as we know, the farthest distance a raiding party reached from the sea was Thronion in Lokris, which was captured in 431 BC by the Athenian admiral Kleopompos, or Kotyra in Lakonia, which was laid waste by the Athenians in 424 BC (Thucydides 2.26.2, 4.56). Both locations were some 10km (6 miles) from the sea, and anything beyond was considered safe from seaborne attacks. Here we should note that the Corinthians suffered little by way of Athenian raiding during the Peloponnesian War, but during the Corinthian War (398–387 BC) their agricultural land was 'laid waste in front of their eyes' (Xenophon *Hellenika* 4.4.1).

## Land bases – *epiteichismoi*

One innovative way in which sea power was employed during the Peloponnesian War was to establish bases on or off the enemy's seacoast. The Athenians established such bases at Pylos in 425 BC, and by

An Etruscan red-figure rhyton in the shape of a trireme's prow. Dated to the 3rd or 2nd century BC, this ritual vessel was found in a tomb at Vulci. It shows clearly the ram and, above on both sides, the laterally projecting *epōtides*, or ear-timbers. (London, British Museum, GR 1849.4-19.4, author's collection)

The Great Harbour at Syracuse, looking south-east from Castello Eurialo. The Syracusans took every advantage of the geography of their harbour, as the confined space made it impossible for the Athenians to exploit their superiority in speed and agility. (Author's collection)

capturing Kythera, the island opposite Lakonia, in 413 BC (Thucydides 4.3–4, 7.26). This type of base was known as an *epiteichismos*, a word that is both striking and technical and best translated as 'fortification-in-enemy-territory'. The establishment of such Athenian bases within Spartan territory stirred up trouble for the Spartans because they led to an increase in helot unrest. Yet such a scheme does not appear to have been part of Perikles' strategy, and the Corinthians first advocated the use of *epiteichismoi* in 432 BC (Thucydides 1.122.1). On the other hand, Perikles only envisaged the use of *epiteichismoi* as a counter-move to any Spartan bases established in Attica (Thucydides 1.142.2–4).

## Periklean strategy

Perikles' main strategic ideas are clear. Like Themistokles before him, Perikles focused more on the navy than the army, and Athens' naval resources were immeasurably superior to its land power. He would

An Attic red-figure stamnos from the necropolis at Vulci. Dated to *circa* 480–470 BC and attributed to the Siren Painter, the scene depicts Odysseus' encounter with the Sirens. The single-banked vessel is shown with a bronze-sheathed ram, clearly delineating her as a warship. (London, British Museum, GR 1842.11-3.31, Esther Carré)

23

evacuate the hinterland of Attica, bring the population into the Long Walls, decline battle with the Spartan army, and rely on the navy to protect Athenian grain supplies and secure the empire on whose resources the expensive naval policy depended. Expenditure on shipbuilding had been counterbalanced by annual savings from the tribute, and enough capital had been reserved, he thought, for a long war, although costs turned out to be heavier than he could have calculated. This is essentially Thucydides' analysis, though he failed to explain what end to the war, other than a stalemate, Perikles wanted or expected.

Though Perikles stressed the importance of sea power (Thucydides 2.13.2, 65.7), he appears not to have fully appreciated its uses. As such he shows absurd complacency, as Thucydides records: 'The destruction of a part of the Peloponnese will be worse for them than the destruction of the whole of Attica would be for us. For they can get no more land without fighting for it, while we have plenty of land both in the islands and on the mainland [i.e. Anatolia]. Such is the power, which control of the sea gives' (Thucydides 1.143.4–5).

A much more fruitful use of sea power is to cut off supplies at their source. There is an implication from Thucydides that Athens thought along these lines for, in 426 BC, it despatched ships to Sicily under Laches and Charoaiades 'to prevent grain being brought in to the Peloponnese from the west' (3.86.2).

The trouble with such a strategy is that it depends upon an enemy being reliant upon seaborne supplies. Athens was certainly dependent on maritime imports, particularly grain from the Black Sea region, and thus its sea power was needed for the protection of its commerce. On the other hand, sea power was of little use if Athens ultimately wished to defeat Sparta, a stalwart land power. Needless to say, Sparta was fully aware of this shortcoming, as well as the fact that Athens was dependent upon seaborne supplies. Archidamos hinted as much in 432 BC when he advocated building up Sparta's navy to disrupt such commerce (Thucydides. 1.81.4). Still, until 413 BC Sparta was unable to match the might of the Athenian navy, and thus it could only despatch its fleets to stir up revolts within the empire (e.g. Chios, Lesbos), or to establish blockades (e.g. the Hellespont). Sparta had never been an important naval power, but the Athenian disaster in Sicily in 413 BC presented it with the opportunity of becoming one.

**Salamis Straits, looking towards Peiraieus from the Paloúkia–Pérama ferry. This narrow ribbon of blue water allowed the Greeks, despite their inferior numbers and heavier triremes, to slog it out with the invading Persian armada and severely maul it. (Author's collection)**

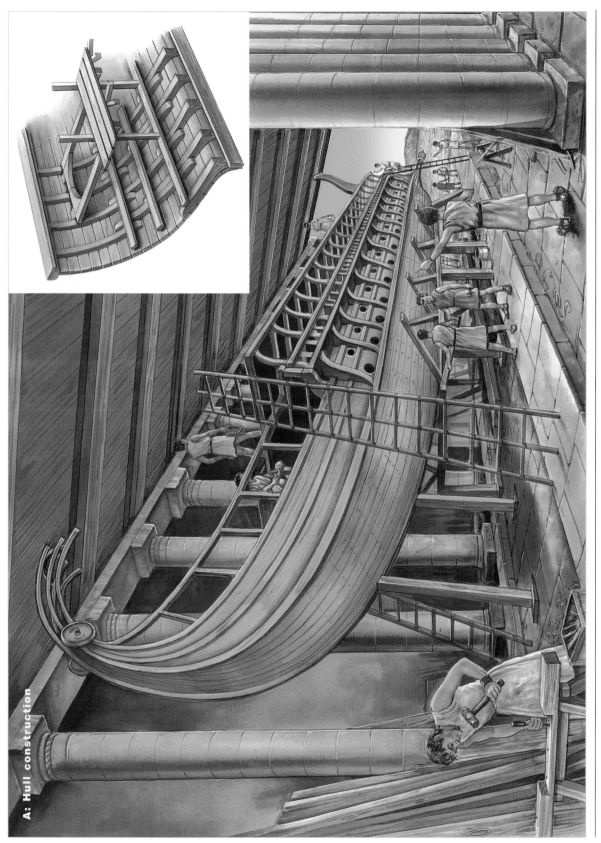

A: Hull construction

A

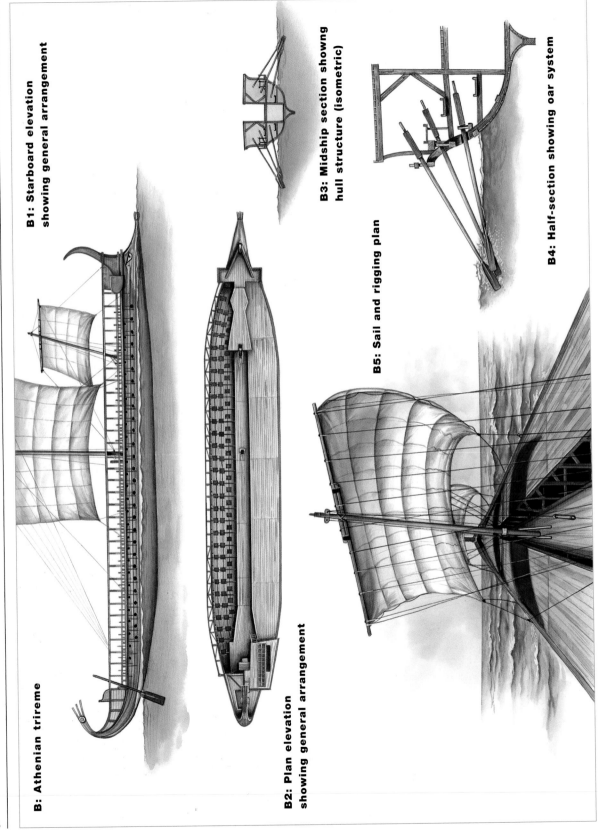

**B: Athenian trireme**

**B1: Starboard elevation showing general arrangement**

**B2: Plan elevation showing general arrangement**

**B3: Midship section showng hull structure (isometric)**

**B4: Half-section showing oar system**

**B5: Sail and rigging plan**

B

C: Ship sheds of Mounychia, Peiraieus

**D: OARSMEN**

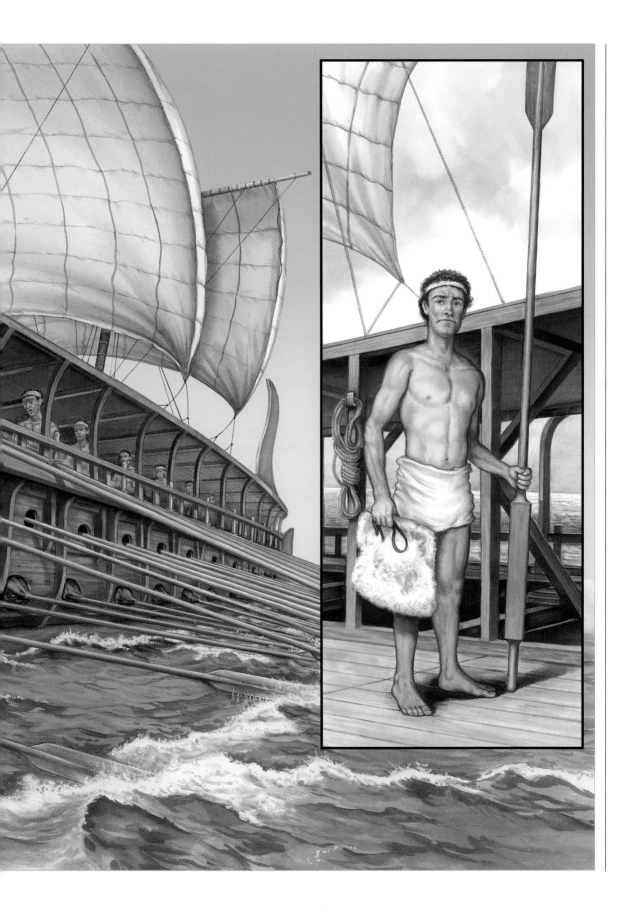

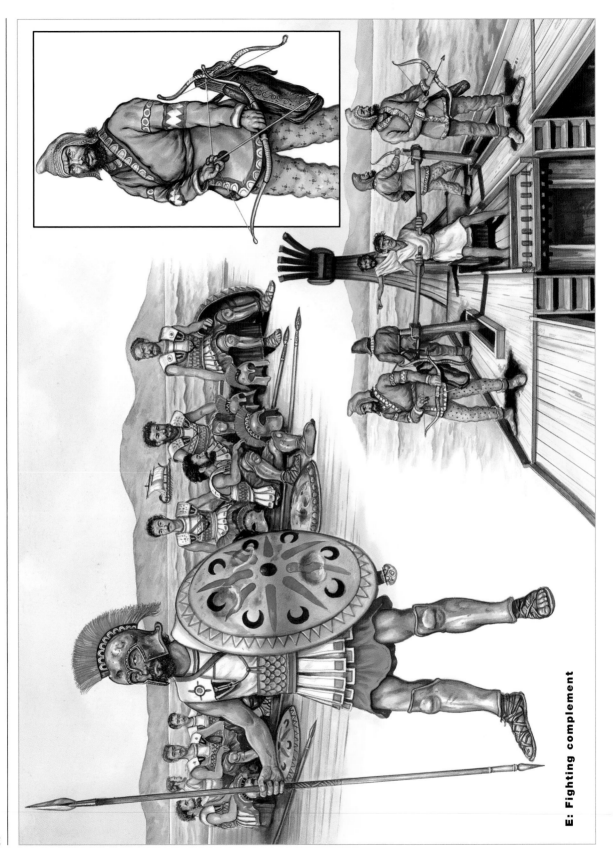

E: Fighting complement

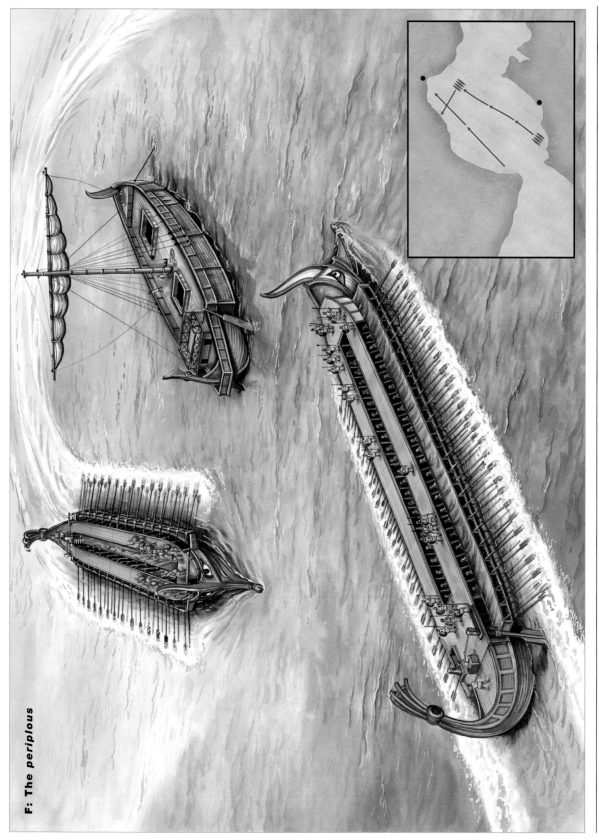

G: The final sea battle in the Great Harbour at Syracuse, 413 BC

Gylippos and the Syracusans trapped the Athenian fleet within the Great Harbour and the besiegers found themselves cut off. This is the entrance to the Great Harbour looking south from Via Eolo, across which the Syracusans slung a boom of chained merchantmen. (Author's collection)

A marble bust of Perikles, a 2nd-century Roman copy from Hadrian's Villa, Tivoli. It was under Perikles that Athens would become the greatest maritime empire that the Mediterranean had ever known. (London, British Museum, GR 1805.7-3.91, author's collection)

In the spring of 413 BC Sparta sent Derkyllidas to the Hellespont in order to bring about the revolt of Abydos, a vassal-state of Athens. Later that year Klearchos sailed with 40 triremes to attempt a blockade of the Hellespont and thus cut Athens off from its Black Sea grain supplies (Thucydides 8.61.1, 80.1). Despite this stratagem, however, Agis of Sparta, who was holding Dekeleia in north-eastern Attica (a classic example of an *epiteichismos*), reckoned it was a waste of time attempting to cut Athens' supply lines when he could still see the grain ships putting into Peiraieus (Xenophon *Hellenika* 1.1.35).

The alternative was to engage Athens on the high seas, but in doing so Sparta was to suffer absolute disaster at sea in both 410 and 406 BC. However, in 405 BC Sparta finally gained the upper hand and its admiral Lysandros resoundingly defeated the Athenians at the engagement off Aigospotami. The following year Lysandros was able to strangle the Athenians into submission, his naval victory having effectively severed their grain supplies from the Black Sea region. So Athens itself became vulnerable to the sea power of its enemies: the state's reliance upon seaborne supply was its Achilles heel. It was to suffer the same fate again in 386 BC (Xenophon *Hellenika* 5.1.28).

# THE ATHENIAN NAVY

Thucydides puts into the mouths of Corcyraean envoys to Athens the following words: 'There are three considerable naval powers in Hellas – Athens, Corcyra, and Corinth' (1.36.3). Indeed, at the outset of the Peloponnesian War the Athenian navy was the largest in the Greek world, with no fewer than 300 triremes 'fit for service' (Thucydides 2.13.8). The nearest rival was the Corcyraean navy, which had 120 triremes (Thucydides 1.25.4, 33.1), and Corcyra was allied to Athens. In addition, Athens could employ ships from Chios and Lesbos; 50 triremes from these two island states, for example, joined in the attack on Epidauros in 430 BC (Thucydides 2.56.2). The Athenians naturally could not man all their ships at any one time – apart from the cost, 300 triremes would have required 60,000 able-bodied seamen. But the existence of this huge number of seaworthy hulls gave them a substantial reserve. The revenue

from the empire also enabled them to accumulate a reserve of 6,000 talents – enough to keep all 300 triremes in operation for 20 months – and imperial tribute came to 600 talents a year (Thucydides 2.13.3).

## When Athena ruled the waves

As there were limits to what could be achieved with sea power, the trireme was essentially designed for battle. The development of the *diekplous* and the *periplous* tactics during the 5th century BC made the Athenian trireme an object of dread. At Sybota the presence of just ten Athenian triremes,

Attic black-figure kylix from the Etruscan burial site at Vulci, dated *circa* 540 BC. On the inside of this cup, painted by Exekias, Dionysos reclines on the deck of a warship armed with a ram. (Munich, Museum Antiker Kleinkunst, 2044, author's collection)

which were supporting the Corcyraean fleet, was enough to frighten the Corinthians into backing away (Thucydides 1.49.3). Four years later, the Athenian admiral Phormio, commanding a squadron of 20 triremes in the Gulf of Corinth, defeated a Peloponnesian fleet of 47 triremes even though the latter had formed a *kuklos* (Thucydides 2.83–84). Again, in 427 BC, 12 Athenian triremes, among which were the sacred triremes *Salaminia* and *Paralos*, outmanoeuvred and outfought 33 Peloponnesian triremes off Corcyra (Thucydides 3.77–78). When an Athenian was asked of his place of birth, he proudly answered: 'From where the fine triremes come' (Aristophanes *Birds* 108). It seems that the superior quality of Athenian ships was well worth boasting about.

### Expenditure

Apart from the cost of building warships, their crews had to be paid. The cost of paying even a single trireme's crew could rise to a talent a month (Thucydides 6.8.1). In Athens the state financed the ship and its crew, but rich citizens paid for the equipment and repairs as one of the liturgies (*triērarchia*). According to the Decree of Themistokles (Fornara 55) the 'qualifications are the possession of land and a house in Attica, children born in wedlock, age not over fifty' (lines 20–23). The number of those wealthy enough to qualify for this public honour at the time of the Peloponnesian War was 400, as mentioned by the 'Old Oligarch' (Pseudo-Xenophon *Athenaion politeia* 3.4).

The *triērarchia* was a brilliant Athenian notion, which shamed the richest citizens into spending their wealth on the state, without the need for taxation. This system allowed the citizen to serve for one year as the *triērarchos* of the vessel he had sponsored. The position brought honour,

**The stern of *Olympias*.** Instead of a rudder hinged on the stern-post, triremes used two steering-oars, one on each side of the stern. Each was attached to a tiller (*oiax*), the ends of which were close together so that the helmsman could work both at once. (Author's collection)

but it also entailed much trouble, risk of life, and often exorbitant financial demands, an aggregation felt to be particularly onerous during the distressing final years of the Peloponnesian War.

To ease things for those eligible, in 408 BC the requirements were slackened by allowing two or more co-sponsors to share service on a trireme (Lysias 32.24, 26, *IG* 1² 1951.79–81). Yet many continued to find the burdens excessively heavy. For instance, in 378 BC about 50 perfectly seaworthy triremes (half of Athens' fleet) lay idle (*anepiklērōtoi*, 'unallotted') because of lack of *triērarchoi* (*IG* 1² 1604). The amount of money involved was, indeed, considerable. For a complete set of equipment, *triērarchoi* were required to pay 2,169 *drachmae* if it included an ordinary, 'heavy' sail (*IG* 2² 1629.667–673), or 2,299 *drachmae* if it included a finer, 'lighter' sail (*IG* 2² 1629.577–584). Other gear included 170 working oars with 30 spares, two steering-oars, two ladders, three poles, as well as diverse bits of tackle and ropes of various thickness and length. Replacement of a hull meant payment of 5,000 *drachmae* (*IG* 2² 1628.353–368), which thus puts the replacement of an entire ship at 7,169 or 7,299 *drachmae*. Towards the end of our period, the value of trireme gear had risen to about 4,100 *drachmae* (*IG* 2² 1631.446–448, 462–466). Little wonder then to see the 4th century orator Lysias pinning on the triremes the epithet 'gluttonous' (fr. 39 Talheim). In another forensic speech (19.29, 42), he describes a man who had been a *triērarchos* for three consecutive years and spent 8,000 *drachmae* (an annual average of 2,666 *drachmae*). There were large costs involved in keeping triremes afloat.

### Downfall of the imperial navy

It is significant that by the summer of 413 BC the Peloponnesian navy was gaining the upper hand. In the Gulf of Corinth off Erinaios, Achaia, 25 Peloponnesian triremes took up station in an anchorage that was crescent-shaped and waited to engage the Athenian fleet stationed at Naupaktos opposite. As the projecting headlands at each side of the

Naupaktos, looking north-west from the town beach. Naupaktos was an Athenian outpost just inside the Gulf of Corinth on its northern shore. At the start of the Peloponnesian War the Athenian admiral Phormio made Naupaktos his base for a blockade of Sparta's ally, Corinth. (Author's collection)

bay protected the wings of the Peloponnesian fleet, the 33 Athenian triremes were forced to engage head-on. Seven Athenian ships were put out of action after being rammed head-on by the Corinthian triremes, which had specially strengthened cat-heads for the purpose of ramming prow to prow (Thucydides 7.34.5). The Athenian rams were designed for a much lighter – if more deadly – task: to penetrate the hull timbers of a trireme from the side.

By the time of the sea battles in the Great Harbour the Syracusans had adopted the Corinthian practice of strengthening their ships at the prow. In addition they also packed the decks of their ships full of marines (Thucydides 7.34, 62). In a letter to the *ekklesia* Nikias, the Athenian commander at Syracuse, complained bitterly of the decline in crews and the acute shortage of experienced personnel to man the fleet (Thucydides 7.13–14). Athens resorted to hiring mercenary crews, yet with financial backing from Persia the Spartans were often able to outbid the Athenian recruiting officers (Xenophon *Hellenika* 1.5.4).

Unfortunately, the naval engagements of the closing stages of the Peloponnesian War are poorly documented. In 411 BC Kynossema was a moral victory for the Athenians who, after the Sicilian disaster, had been afraid of the Peloponnesian navy with its Syracusan allies, 'but now they got rid of their feelings of inferiority and ceased to believe that the enemy was worth anything at sea' (Thucydides 8.104–106). Kyzikos in 410 BC was a scrambling fight along the Hellespontine coast (Xenophon *Hellenika* 1.1.1–18). Off Arginousai in 406 BC the 120-strong Peloponnesian fleet, 'with their more skilful crews', drew up line abreast 'so as to be able to execute the *diekplous* and the *periplous*', while the Athenians, lacking their former confidence, formed a double line abeam with their 143 triremes (Xenophon *Hellenika* 1.6.26–34). The engagement off Aigospotami in 405 BC was an anti-climax as the Athenian crews were mostly caught ashore, only nine of the 180 triremes, including Konon's flagship, being manned and ready for action (Xenophon *Hellenika* 2.1.20–29).

### Revival in the 4th century

In 404 BC Athens had been forced to surrender all but 12 ships of its navy to Sparta (Xenophon *Hellenika* 2.2.20), yet during the course of the 4th century BC, the Athenian navy far surpassed its 5th-century strength. In 357 BC, the navy numbered 283 triremes, but four years later it had been enlarged to 349. In 330 BC, the total had climbed to 392 triremes plus 18 quadriremes (*tetrēreis*). Four years later there were 360 triremes and 50 quadriremes, while in the following year seven quinqueremes (*pentēreis*) had been added to that number. Finally, in 323 BC, the navy had a total of 315 triremes and 50 quadriremes.

Of course, quality ranks higher than quantity, and the fleets launched in the 4th century BC were in no way inferior to those that cruised up and down the Aegean in the days of empire. Before 357 BC, all triremes were simply classed into 'new', 'old' and an intermediate category without a specific label (*IG* 2² 1604). From that date, however, triremes were divided into four ratings: 'firsts', 'seconds', 'thirds' and 'select' (*IG* 2² 1611.73, 96, 147, 157). The latter, also called *tachunautousai*, 'fast-sailing' (*IG* 2² 1623.276–308), were lightly built, especially agile vessels used on special missions such as spearheading surprise attacks in battle, or running down pirates. Together with the 'firsts' they formed the élite of the navy. Next to them came the amply serviceable 'seconds'. The lowest rating, the 'thirds', were numerically insignificant. In Zea, the larger of the two military harbours at Peiraieus, there were about 30 'firsts', 46 'seconds', as many as 50 'select' (10, 16 and 17 percent of the total of 283 triremes in 357 BC), but only eight 'thirds'.

Quarterdeck and helmsman's station on *Olympias*. Standing just below the enthroned *triērarchos*, the helmsman would operate the two tillers (*oiākos*), which were attached to the steering-oars. A lifelong mariner and the most important man on board, a skilled helmsman could steer a ship to victory. (Author's collection)

Yet the sad epilogue of Athenian sea power was written in 322 BC. In an engagement off Amorgos, the Athenian fleet suffered a crushing defeat by the numerically superior Macedonian forces (Diodoros 18.5.8–9, *FGrHist* 239B9 = Harding 1). The eclipse was as sudden as it was dramatic. What the Macedonian admiral Kleitos really managed to accomplish was to strike a lethal blow not on a disintegrating giant, but on one of the most distinguished naval powers in the history of the Mediterranean.

## OLYMPIAS

*Olympias* is a full-scale, painstaking reconstruction of an Athenian trireme of the 4th century BC. It measures 36.8m (120ft) in overall length, 5.45m (18ft) across outriggers, 3.65m (12ft) beam, and 42 tonnes (41.3 tons) total displacement. It was built in Greece to a design worked out by John Coates, a former Chief Naval Architect for the Ministry of Defence, taking into consideration ancient evidence meticulously researched by Professor John Morrison, former President of Wolfson College, University of Cambridge. The hull was of shell-first, mortise-and-tenon construction typical of Mediterranean ships of antiquity. *Olympias* was commissioned into the Hellenic Navy on 27 June 1987, and under its aegis five successive series of sea trials were carried out in 1987, 1988, 1990, 1992 and 1994. She is now displayed on dry land at Flísvos Marina at Palaió Fáliro, the marine branch of the Naval Museum of Greece, Peiraieus.

*Askōmata* were leather sleeves through which the *thalamioi* worked their oars. They were used to prevent water coming through the lower and larger row of oar-ports when the sea was choppy. Immediately above these two *askōmata* are two *zugioi* oar-ports, and above those two *thranitai* tholepins. (Author's collection)

## Performance under oar

The best speed attained by *Olympias* in reported trials is 7.1 knots (13km/h, 8mph) for a period of just under five minutes. The best-recorded measured mile was covered at 7.05 knots with a flying start. Based on Xenophon's statement that the journey from Byzantium on the northern shore of the Bosporos, to Herakleia on the southern coast of the Black Sea took 'a long day's voyage for a trireme under oar' (*Anabasis* 6.4.2), it is estimated that an Athenian trireme could maintain a cruising speed of about 8.6 knots (16km/h, 10mph). The distance from Byzantium is taken to be 129 nautical miles (239km/148 miles).

However, a major problem for the crew of modern varsity rowers is a chronic lack of space for movement. To obtain the best performance, each rower should be able to reach forward with his/her arm straight at each catch, and move from the hips, using additional force from the leg muscles. This is, of course, greatly helped by the sliding seats of modern racing eights. But on *Olympias* the seats are fixed, and the total horizontal movement of the rower's hands is limited to about 85cm (33in.). This means that any rower more than about 1.72m (5ft 6in.) tall cannot straighten his/her arms at the catch without hitting the back of the rower

in front. So instead of relaxing his/her arm muscles, the rower has to waste energy in keeping them taut.

A crew of ancient Athenian oarsmen, none of whom was over 1.67m (5ft 5in.) tall, and who had trained together as a team for months or even years, might well have achieved 9.5 or even 10 knots (17.5–18.5km/h, 10.8–11.4mph), whereas the volunteer crews, many of them over 1.82m (5ft 10in.) tall, were unable to use their full potential. Another discomfort was the heat and the lack of ventilation in the bowels of the ship. Each of *Olympias'* crew was drinking a litre of water for each hour of rowing, a rate of consumption that would require 1.7 tonnes (1.6 tons) of water in a ten-hour rowing day (Morrison-Coates 2000: 238).

The amount of water needed to prevent dehydration caused by sustained exertion can be reduced for some hours if it contains sodium and a food that can be absorbed quickly. Triremes probably carried salt for that purpose, but glucose was not known until modern times. The only reference to food taken during a prolonged passage under oar is by Thucydides, who wrote, 'they pulled and ate at the same time, barley bread mixed with wine and olive oil' (3.49.3). The ancient Athenians, with their lower body mass, were probably made of sterner stuff than their modern counterparts, who are mostly trained for sprint racing.

### Timber

As the types of wood used in Athenian triremes are nowadays difficult to obtain in the eastern Mediterranean, the nearest equivalents available from elsewhere were used – durable iroko instead of oak for the principle structural members of the hull, the keel and the timbers of the stem and ram, and oak only for the tenons joining the planks and for the dowel-pins that held them in place. Douglas fir was used for the shell of the hull instead of the botanically authentic species such as silver fir, larch or several of the many pines that grow around the Mediterranean and Black Sea. The same species was also employed for the oars used in the first trials, although this raised a problem as it is not a true fir but a rather heavier wood, which made rowing more difficult. Even so, the hull of *Olympias* has positive buoyancy, and would not sink if holed.

# BIBLIOGRAPHY

Cawkwell, G. L., 'Athenian naval power in the fourth century', *Classical Quarterly*, 34 (1984), pp.334–345

Dow, S., 'The purported Decree of Themistokles: stele and inscription', *American Journal of Archaeology*, 66 (1962), pp.353–368

Gabrielsen, V., *Financing the Athenian Fleet: Public Taxation and Social Relations*, John Hopkins University Press, Baltimore (1994)

Hammond, N. G. L., 'The battle of Salamis', *Journal of Hellenic Studies*, 76 (1956), pp.32–54

– 'On Salamis', *American Journal of Archaeology*, 64 (1960), pp.367–368

– 'The narrative of Herodotos VII and the decree of Themistocles at Troezen', *Journal of Hellenic Studies*, 102 (1982), pp.75–93

– 'The manning of the fleet in the decree of Themistokles', *Phoenix*, 40 (1986), pp.143–148

Jameson, M. H., 'A decree of Themistokles from Troezen', *Hesperia*, 29 (1960), pp.198–223

– 'A revised text of the decree of Themistokles from Troezen', *Hesperia*, 31 (1962), pp.310–315

– 'The provisions for mobilisation in the decree of Themistokles', *Historia*, 12 (1963), pp.385–404

Landels, J. G., *Engineering in the Ancient World*, Constable, London, (1978, revised 2000)

Lazenby, J. F., 'The *diekplous*', *Greece & Rome*, 34 (1987), pp.169–177

– 'Aischylos and Salamis', *Hermes*, 116 (1988), pp.168–185

– *The Defence of Greece, 490–479 BC*, Aris & Phillips, Warminster (1993)

– *The Peloponnesian War: A Military Study*, Routledge, London (2004)

Lewis, D. M., 'Notes on the Decree of Themistocles', *Classical Quarterly*, 11 (1961), pp. 61–66

Morrison, J. S., 'The Greek ships at Salamis and the *diekplous*', *Journal of Hellenic Studies*, 111 (1991), pp.196–200

Morrison, J. S., and J. F. Coates, *The Athenian Trireme: The History and Reconstruction of an Ancient Greek Warship*, CUP, Cambridge (1986, 2nd ed. 2000)

Pritchett, W. K., 'Towards a restudy of the battle of Salamis', *American Journal of Archaeology*, 63 (1959), pp.251–262

– 'Herodotus and the Themistokles decree', *American Journal of Archaeology*, 66 (1962), pp.43–47

Robertson, N., 'The decree of Themistocles in its contemporary setting', *Phoenix*, 36 (1982), pp.1–44

Shaw, J. T. (ed.), *The Trireme Project. Operational Experience 1987–90. Lessons Learnt*, Oxbow Monograph 31, Oxford (1993)

Tilley, A. F., *Seafaring in the Ancient World: New Thoughts on Triremes and Other Ancient Ships*, BAR International Series 1268, Oxford (2004)

Wallinga, H. T., *Ships and Sea-power Before the Great Persian War: The Ancestry of the Ancient Trireme*, E. J. Brill, Leiden (1993)

Whitehead, I., 'The *periplous*', *Greece & Rome*, 34 (1987), pp.178–185

## Ancient authors

Only the most frequently cited ancient authors are listed here. Further details about them, and information about other sources, is most conveniently available in *The Oxford Classical Dictionary* (3rd edition). In the following notes Penguin denotes Penguin Classics, and Loeb denotes Loeb Classical Library (*www.hup.harvard.edu/loeb*).

### Aischylos (525–*c.*456 BC)

A tragedian from Athens, Aischylos fought at the battle of Marathon and his brother Kynegeiros was killed in the aftermath. His total output is variously stated at between 70 and 90 plays, of which only seven have survived. As Aischylos was responsible for the introduction of a second actor, thereby allowing for true dialogue, he is generally regarded as the real founder of Greek tragedy. His most important play for our purposes is the *Persians* (*Persai*), which deals with the Persian naval defeat at Salamis in September 480 BC, at which Aischylos himself was probably present. In general, his plots tend to be characterized not by abrupt changes of direction, but by a build-up of tension and expectation of a climax anticipated by the audience. The *Persians* is available both in a Penguin and Loeb editions.

### Herodotos (*c.*484–430 BC)

An Ionian historian born in Doric-speaking Halikarnassos, Herodotos, the so-called 'Father of History' spent much of his life in Athens. He was, in fact, the first to make events of the past the subject of research and verification, which is what the word *historíe* meant. His work, in truth a masterpiece, is the chief source for the events of the Graeco-Persian Wars at the turn of the 5th century BC, but contains much else, including wonderful accounts of various cultures, myths and sights. If we believe what he says, he travelled extensively in the known world of the Greeks, from the northern shores of the Black Sea to Elephantine on the First Cataract of the Nile, and from the 'heel' of Italy to western Iran. We have no means of checking most of this, but he was a terrific collector and teller of marvellous stories (*logoi*). The *Histories* is available in Penguin edition.

### Thucydides (*c.*460–400 BC)

An Athenian, Thucydides wrote an unfinished account of the Pelopon-nesian War (431–404 BC), the monumental conflict fought between Athens and Sparta and their respective allies. He served as a general in 424 BC and was subsequently exiled at the end of that year following an unlucky expedition in northern Greece against the very able Spartan commander Brasidas. During his exile in Thrace, where his family had connections and property, he compiled his history of the war. His exile, he claims, gave him opportunities for appreciating the point of view of each of the combatants. An unfinished work (it breaks off amid the events of 411 BC), *A History of the Peloponnesian War* is our most important single source for the 5th century BC. Thucydides obviously was an eyewitness to many of the events and personalities he describes, or at least was able to gain information from reliable sources. His is a densely written narrative, however, which does not furnish us with alternative accounts, unlike the style of Herodotos. It is therefore sometimes easy to mistake the author's account of events as an authoritative narrative. The speeches are a particular problem. Thucydides says he wrote what he could remember of the speeches that he heard, but also wrote what seems likely to have been said on an occasion. This important work is available both in Penguin and Loeb editions, although the translation by Richard Crawley in the Everyman's Library edition is much better.

### Xenophon (*c.*428–355 BC)

An Athenian-born soldier-of-fortune, historian and essayist, Xenophon is an extremely useful, though generally much underrated, author. His extant works are available in Penguin and Loeb editions and include accounts of the Spartan constitution, as well as his own military exploits as a mercenary. Of importance to us is his *Hellenika* (published by Penguin as *A History of My Own Times*), a narrative history of Greece from 411 to 362 BC. Of significance is the fact that the events narrated occurred in the author's own lifetime. Moreover, he was present (accompanying his close friend Agesilaos, king of Sparta) during several of the campaigns he describes. His other extant works also include the brilliant account of his adventures with the Ten Thousand (*Anabasis*).

The quarterdeck ladder and gangway on *Olympias*. The bo'sun stood in the gangway, midway along, and called out instructions to the oarsmen. He had the help of the bow officer, while a piper kept time on a shrill double pipe. (Author's collection)

# COLOUR PLATE COMMENTARY

## A: HULL CONSTRUCTION

The prime considerations of the Athenian shipbuilder were legroom and lightness. The total space occupied by the 170 oarsmen had to be the very minimum without interfering with their rowing. The trireme hull, therefore, was slender, long, and of shallow draught relative to its displacement volume.

Built shell-first, the adjacent planks of the hull were firmly joined together edge-to-edge by large numbers of closely spaced tenons fitted tightly into individual mortises sunk into the plank edges, and then, when the close-fitting seam was finished, the tenons were pegged in place. For strength, tenons were made of a selected hardwood, usually Turkish oak. The dowel pins securing the tenons were made from more common oak.

Transverse framing was fitted as the shell was built up. Framing was secured to the shell planking by copper spikes, which had tapered square shanks and large, shallow-domed heads. These spikes are driven up pine dowels into prepared holes bored through plank and framing. The points of the spikes were clenched over and driven back into the face of the framing.

Aerial view of modern Peiraieus, the port of Athens, looking north-west. The larger commercial harbour, Kantharos, is top left. Zea and Mounychia, the two smaller harbours with the ship sheds, are seen centre and right respectively and served as the military harbours of ancient Athens. (Author's collection)

## B: ATHENIAN TRIREME

| | |
|---|---|
| **Length:** | 36.80m (120ft) |
| **Beam (hull):** | 3.65m (12ft) |
| **Beam (outriggers):** | 5.45m (18ft) |
| **Draught:** | 1.20m (4ft) |
| **Total displacement:** | 42 tonnes (41.3 tons) |

**Oarsmen (*nautai*) 170:**
   62 upper oarsmen (*thranitai*)
   54 middle oarsmen (*zugioi*)
   54 lower oarsmen (*thalamioi*)
**Armed men 14:**
   10 citizen marines (*epibatai*)
   4 mercenary archers (*toxotai*)
**Specialist seamen 16:**
   1 sea-captain (*triērarchos*)
   1 helmsman (*kubernētēs*)
   1 bo'sun (*keleustēs*)
   1 bow officer (*prōratēs*)
   1 shipwright (*naupēgos*)
   1 double-pipe player (*aulētēs*)
   10 deck-hands
**Crew total: 200**

**B1:** Starboard elevation showing general arrangement.
**B2:** Plan elevation showing general arrangement.
**B3:** Midship section showing hull structure (isometric).
**B4:** Half-section showing oar system.
**B5:** Sail and rigging plan.

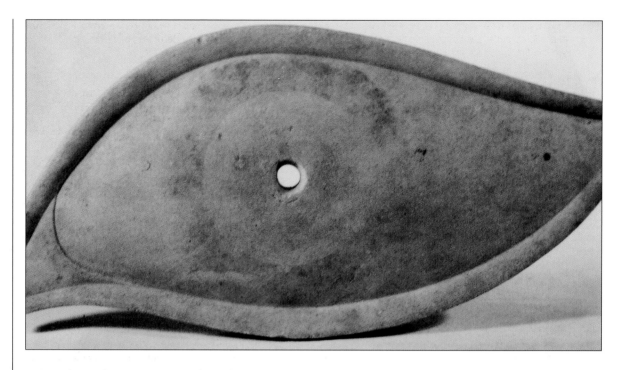

A talismanic eye from Zea, Peiraieus (c.500 BC). Made of Parian marble, this once decorated a trireme. The eyelids, eyeball and corners of the eye are in relief. Three concentric rings painted in shades of yellow ochre and red represent the iris. (Peiraieus, Archaeological Museum, 3640, Esther Carré)

## C: SHIP SHEDS OF MOUNYCHIA, PEIRAIEUS

To minimize rotting and attacks of the *teredo navalis* woodworm, triremes were not only coated with pitch, but were kept out of the water and protected from the weather when not in use (mainly in winter) in a position where they could be rapidly available when needed. At Peiraieus, the two smaller harbours (Zea and Mounychia) and part of the larger commercial harbour (Kantharos) were reserved for warships.

In the military harbours the most distinctive features were the ship sheds, which numbered 372 by the second half of the 4th century BC (*IG* 2² 1627.398–405). Almost completely occupying the shoreline of the two smaller harbours, there were 196 in Zea and 82 in Mounychia, long narrow structures sloping down to the water, roofed in pairs. Here we see those in Mounychia, below the hill of the same name, which was sacred to Artemis and made a fine fortress that commanded a wide view of land and sea.

The ship sheds have a continuous back wall, with rows of un-fluted stone columns running down to the sea forming the partitions between slips and supporting a gabled roof over each pair. At intervals a solid wall divides the ship sheds into groups. The fairly open structure provides the ventilation necessary to dry out the ships, but security and fire-prevention also had to be considered. The actual slips are low platforms 3m (10ft) wide cut in the bedrock, flat in cross-section and sloping seawards. Timber runners are laid on the slips, which have a gradient of 1 in 10. The ship sheds are 40m (131ft) long and have a clear width between the rows of columns of around 6m (20ft).

## D: OARSMEN

The fundamental innovation of the trireme was that, since the ship was no more than 37m (120ft) long, the oarsmen were not arranged in straight lines, but in three staggered banks. This arrangement thus accomplished the threefold aim of a) not hampering rowing operations, b) not needing excessively high freeboard and c) limiting the vessel to a reasonable length. The cramped and poorly ventilated world of the oarsmen was permeated by the pungent odours of pine resin, mutton tallow, sweat and flatulence, and occasionally of blood and vomit.

The oar was some 4.5m (15ft) in length. A short but wide oar blade was preferable to a long narrow one at all three levels of a trireme. Consisting of a separate piece spliced and riveted on to the shaft, the blade, for economy in wood and ease of manufacture, was flat rather than spoon-shaped. The handgrip at the butt was long enough for the oarsman's hands to be kept about two hands' breadths apart. The oar-loop, which lashed the oar to the tholepin, took the whole strain of the pull. In the *Odyssey* (4.782) Homer refers to oar-loops of leather, but experience in *Olympias* has shown that leather oar-loops stretch and break. Rope grommets are better. Whichever option was used, they had to be greased from time to time with mutton tallow.

## E: FIGHTING COMPLEMENT

The *epibatēs* (left) is a citizen-hoplite in his early twenties. His panoply (*panoplia*), weighing anywhere from 22.7 to 31.7kg (50–70lb), consists of a shield (*aspis*) some 90cm (35 ½in.) in diameter, a bronze helmet, a bronze or linen corselet and bronze greaves.

Built on a wooden core, the shield is faced with a thin layer of stressed bronze and backed by leather. Because of its great weight, (6.8–9.1kg or 15–20lb), the shield was carried by an arrangement of two handles; the armband (*porpax*) in the centre through which the forearm passed, and the handgrip (*antilabē*) at the rim. Held across the chest, it covered the hoplite from chin to knee. However, being clamped to the left arm, it only offered protection to his left-hand side.

Above the flat, broad rim of the shield, a hoplite's head was fully protected by a bronze helmet, the Corinthian helmet being by far the most common style. This was fashioned from a single sheet of bronze that covered the entire face, leaving only the eyes clear. The stress on protection seriously impaired both hearing and vision, so out of battle it could be pushed to the back of the head to leave the face uncovered.

A linen corselet (*linothōrax*) protected the torso. This was built up of multiple layers of linen glued together to form a stiff shirt, about half a centimetre thick. Below the waist it was cut into strips (*pteruges*) for ease of movement, with a second layer of *pteruges* being fixed behind the first, thereby covering the gaps between them. Finally, a pair of bronze greaves (*knemides*) protected the lower legs, which clipped neatly round the calves, held by their own flexibility.

The weapon *par excellence* of the hoplite was the long-thrusting spear (*doru*); some 2 to 2.5m in length (7–9ft), made of ash and equipped with a bronze or iron spearhead and bronze butt-spike, affectionately known as the 'lizard-sticker' (*sauroter*). A short iron sword (*kopis*) was also carried, along with a heavy, leaf-shaped blade designed for slashing, but this was very much a secondary weapon.

The Scythian *toxotēs* (inset), a steppe-dweller from north of the Black Sea and recruited as a mercenary, is gaily clothed in a patterned, loose-fitting tunic with sleeves and trousers, and wears a soft cap of leather. He is armed with a composite bow, a dagger and the *sagaris*, or battle-axe. His *gorytos*, or bow-case is ornamented with painted patterns and contains a spare bow and supply of arrows. He uses the Mediterranean release, whereby the bowstring is drawn back to the chin or chest by the tips of three fingers, with the arrow lightly held like a cigarette, if held at all, between the first and second fingers. The fourth finger and thumb are not used. This technique required the use of a leather bracer on the left forearm, the bow being held in the left hand, to protect it from the backlash of the bowstring. Leather 'shooting tabs' to protect the archer's fingers from the bowstring were also employed. Scythians had a reputation as formidable archers and, by all accounts, they deserved it.

## F: THE *PERIPLOUS*

Based on Thucydides 2.91, this reconstruction shows an Athenian trireme, having performed the *periplous*, preparing to ram a pursuing Leukadian vessel amidships. Eleven Athenian triremes had dashed for Naupaktos with 20 'fast ships' from the Peloponnesian fleet in hot pursuit. Ten of the Athenians made it safely into harbour, and took station near a temple of Apollo, with prows facing outwards, ready to fight. But the last Athenian vessel, finding itself closely followed by a Leukadian trireme, rounded a merchantman anchored off shore and rammed the Leukadian amidships. This caused panic among the remaining pursuing ships, and some dropped oars to let the rest catch up – a foolish thing to do with the enemy so close, as Thucydides said (2.91.4) – while others ran aground in ignorance of the coast. Encouraged by this, the other Athenian ships swept out to re-engage, and after a brief resistance, the Peloponnesians fled, losing six vessels in the process.

## G: THE FINAL SEA BATTLE IN THE GREAT HARBOUR AT SYRACUSE, 413 BC

The largest single expedition that Athens mounted in the Peloponnesian War was to Sicily in 415 BC, consisting of 134 triremes. Reinforcements of 73 triremes followed the next year. In the first sea battle the Syracusans manned 76 triremes. Yet in spite of their advantage in numbers and skill, poor leadership meant that the Athenian armada was trapped in the Great Harbour, where their skill could not be exercised. The outcome in 413 BC was to be a total disaster.

Based on Thucydides 7.70, this reconstruction shows the first impetus of the Athenian attack, which carried them through the Syracusan vessels guarding the boom across the harbour mouth. The Athenians began loosening the chained merchantmen, but then other Syracusan warships joined in from all directions and the fighting became general throughout the harbour. Thucydides emphasizes that it was a harder sea-fight than any of the previous ones, but despite the best efforts of the Athenian helmsmen, because there were so many ships crammed in such a confined space, there were few opportunities to manoeuvre-and-ram, backing water (*anakrousis*) and breaking through the enemy line (*diekplous*) being impossible. Instead, accidental collisions were numerous, leading to fierce fights across decks and much confusion. In other words, this was an engagement in which Athenian skill was nullified.

The 'Two Thrones' of Xerxes, as seen from ancient Salamis town. On this 70m (230ft) high eminence, the Great King established his command post. Here was set the famous golden throne, above the uncompleted mole from which he had intended to bridge the sea to Salamis. (Author's collection)

# INDEX